THE RISE AND FALL OF ANCIENT GREECE

History 3rd Grade
Children's History Books

BABY PROFESSOR

EDUCATION KIDS

Speedy Publishing LLC

40 E. Main St. #1156

Newark, DE 19711

www.speedypublishing.com

Copyright 2017

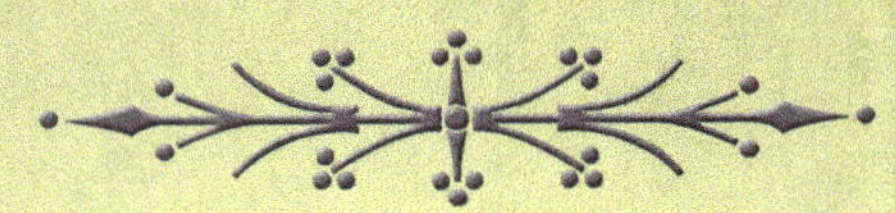

In this book, we're going to cover a brief history of Ancient Greece and the factors that led up to the fall of this great civilization, which still has an impact on our world today. So, let's get right to it!

A BRIEF TIMELINE OF ANCIENT GREECE

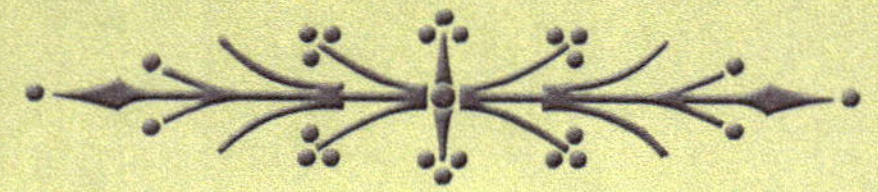

The history of Ancient Greece falls into three major time periods. The first period was the Archaic Period, which was from 800 Bc to 480 Bc. The next period was the Classical Period, which occurred from 480 Bc to 323 Bc. The third period was the Hellenistic Period, which lasted from 323 Bc to 146 Bc. It was during this period that Greece was conquered by the Romans.

MAJOR EVENTS DURING THE ARCHAIC PERIOD (800 BC TO 480 BC)

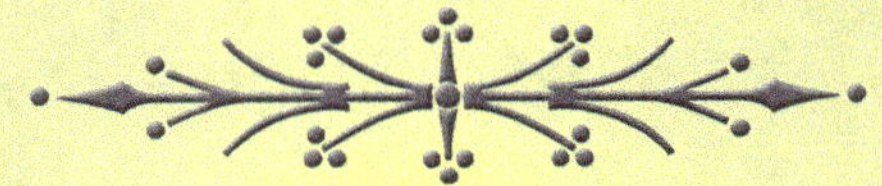

Around 776 BC, the very first Olympic Games were held to honor the Greek god named Zeus. The games took place every four years. The Olympic Games we have today are based on these ancient games.

The city-states of Greece were constantly at war
with each other and eventually this unrest led to
the weakening of their civilization. In 757 BC, the

First Messenian War started. It was the first of many wars
between the city-states of Sparta and Messenia.

Around this time, the author Homer began to write two epic poems called the Iliad and the Odyssey. Over time, these poems became the most famous writings in Greek literature. They still have an influence in modern literature today.

In 621 BC, a lawyer by the name of Draco introduced new laws in the city-state of Athens. These laws were very strict and offenses were punishable by death.

These were called the Draconian laws. Today the word "draconian" means excessively hard or severe.

In 600 BC, the first Greek coins were minted and in 570 BC, the Greek mathematician Pythagoras was born. He would be responsible for major advances not only in mathematics, but also in science and philosophy. The Pythagorean Theorem in geometry is named for him.

Around 508 BC, democratic rule was introduced in the city-state of Athens. One of the great achievements of Greek culture, democracy is the form of government used in many countries today, including the United States.

MAJOR EVENTS DURING THE CLASSICAL PERIOD (480 BC TO 323 BC)

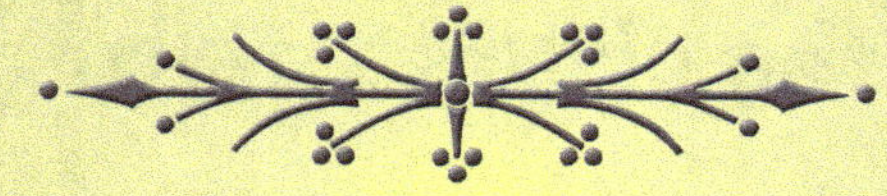

In 490 BC, the Greeks fought the Persians. This conflict became known as the Greek-Persian Wars and its two major battles were the Battle of Marathon and the Battle of Salamis. After much fighting, the Greeks were victorious and the Persians retreated.

Around 468 BC, the writer Sophocles began to write plays, and theater performances became very popular in Greece. In 432 BC, the temple to the goddess Athena called the Parthenon was completed on the Acropolis in Athens. Ruins of this beautiful building still survive today and its architecture still influences modern architectural designs.

Wars between the city-states of
Sparta and Athens erupted in 431 Bc.
The wars lasted about 27 years. Sparta
was eventually victorious but these
Peloponnesian Wars weakened the
civilization. In 399 BC, the famous Greek
philosopher Socrates was sentenced to
death. It was thought that his teachings
were corrupting young students since
he was asking them to question the
existence of the gods the Greeks
believed in at that time.

A student of Socrates, the famous Greek philosopher Plato began the Academy in 386 BC, which was the first school of higher learning in the Western world. Aristotle, the famous philosopher and scientist, became the tutor for the king's son, named Alexander, in 342 Bc. Alexander would soon become king and be known as Alexander the Great.

In 336 BC, King Philip of Macedon was assassinated and young Alexander grabbed power and became king of Greece at age 19. Three years later he started his conquests by defeating the Persians and in 332 Bc he conquered Egypt and began a new capital there called Alexandria, named for him. Over the next few years, he grew his empire and began to conquer Persia on his way to India.

MAJOR EVENTS DURING THE HELLENISTIC PERIOD (323 BC TO 146 BC)

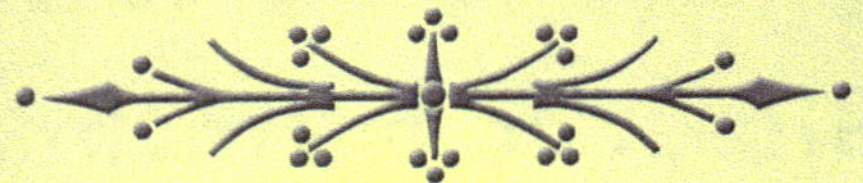

Because Alexander the Great had conquered so many different cultures, the Hellenistic Period was a time when the culture created by the Greeks was mixed with the cultures of Egypt, Persia, and Asia.

This wonderful mixture of cultures created many discoveries and advances in philosophy, astronomy, physics, and mathematics. In 300 BC, the Greek mathematician Euclid wrote the Elements. This famous mathematical work is the basis for Euclidean geometry.

The Hellenistic period also marked the decline of Ancient Greece. In 323 BC, Alexander the Great dies. The civilization of the Ancient Romans began to gain power. Over a century and a half, the Roman Empire became dominant and the Romans conquered Greece in 146 Bc. Fortunately for us, the Romans admired many of the aspects of Greek culture so instead of abandoning this culture, they just brought it into their own.

THE FALL OF GREEK CIVILIZATION

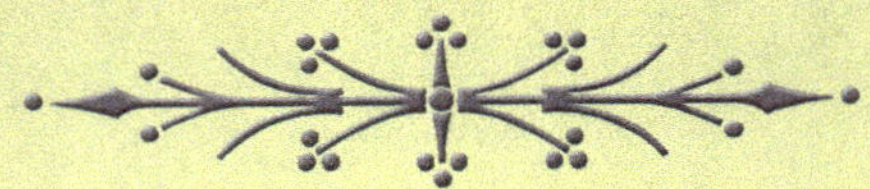

Ancient Greece was an important civilization in the world for centuries. The Greeks made incredible advances in science, philosophy, and the arts. Eventually, their constant internal wars weakened them and made them susceptible to a takeover by Italy. The Romans were the new power in the Mediterranean.

KING PHILIP II OF MACEDON

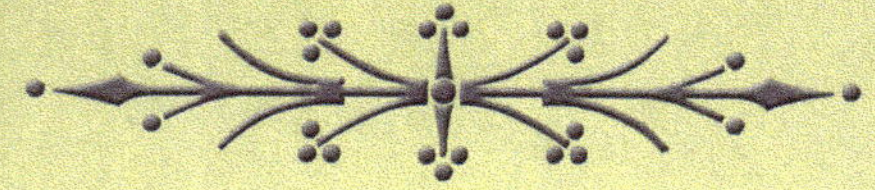

Wars between the city-states known as Athens, Thebes, Corinth, and Sparta made Greece weaker. King Philip II from the region of northern Greece known as Macedon, gained power and in 338 Bc he took control of the cities of Athens and Thebes and brought most of Greece under his government.

KING ALEXANDER THE GREAT

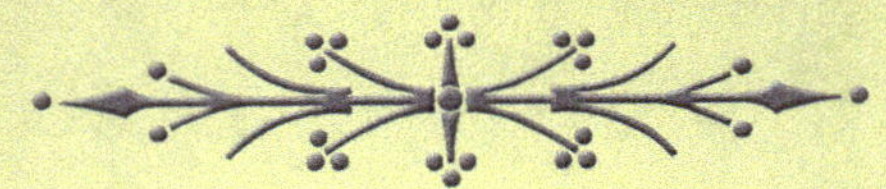

Alexander the Great, the son of King Philip II, grabbed the throne after his father's assassination. Inspired by Homer's great epic poems, Alexander became a great conquering general and won wars on the lands of all neighboring countries between Greece and India, including the great civilization of Egypt.

THE DEATH OF ALEXANDER THE GREAT

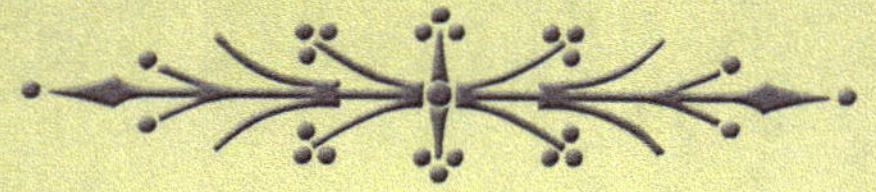

Alexander became very ill at the age of 32. After suffering a high fever for ten days, he passed away. After he died, Greece was divided. His generals took control over different divisions and these new divisions immediately began to fight.

D·O·M·SVB·INVOC·S·M·MAGDALENAE
LA MADELEINE

Although the Greek culture had become dominant throughout the world, politically they were divided. The city-states in Greece began to lose power and the cities of Greek culture and seats of its power were now in Alexandria in Egypt as well as in Antioch and Ephesus in Turkey.

THE RISE OF THE ROMAN EMPIRE

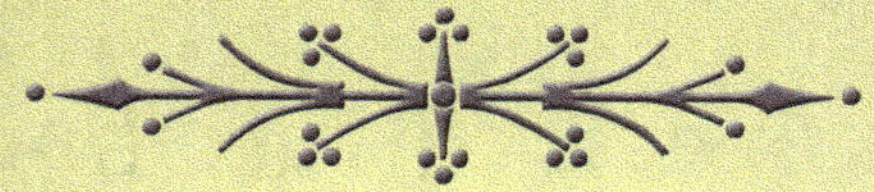

As the civilization of the Greeks was declining, the Romans in Italy were becoming more powerful. The citizens of Greece and its government could see this happening and knew that Rome was a threat.

In 215 BC, regions of Greece joined with Carthage to fight against Rome. The Romans began war with Macedonia and conquered this northern region. They won both the Battle of Cynoscephalae and of Pydna over the course of thirty years.

THE BATTLE OF CORINTH

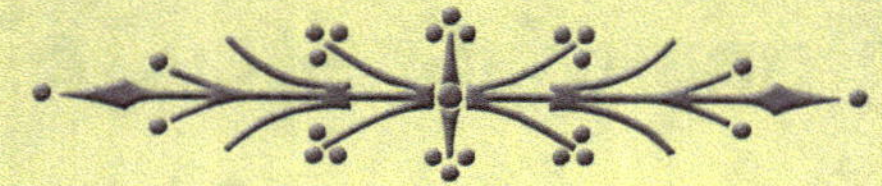

Twenty-two years after the Battle of Pydna, the Romans finally completed their conquest of Greece in 146 BC. To set an example, they completely leveled and looted the great city of Corinth.

This caused fear among the Greek citizens and from this point forward, Greece was governed by the Romans. However, the Romans admired and respected

Greek culture, so they absorbed the culture instead
of destroying it.

FACTORS THAT LED TO THE END OF THE GREEK CIVILIZATION

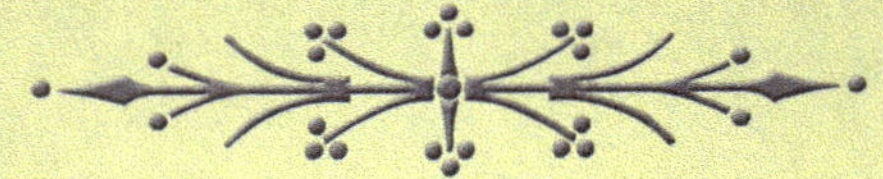

There were multiple factors that brought about the end of Greek civilization. Greece was organized as city-states and they were constantly fighting with each other and switching loyalties. This unrest made it hard for them to unite against Rome. The poor citizens of Greece started to struggle against the wealthy, upper classes.

Even though Alexander had conquered other countries and brought them under the Greek government, they weren't loyal to Greece or its city-states. As the Roman Civilization grew in power and wealth, they were stronger than any of the individual city-states of Greece.

Without one strong leader as they had had in Alexander, power was divided among the military generals and other rulers. This division of power made Greece more vulnerable to an outside attack from the powerful Roman Empire. The Romans had a new way of organized fighting that was called "maniple." This fighting method was more flexible compared to the straight military formations used by the Greeks. This new fighting formation gave the Romans an advantage during their battles.

LIFE IN GREECE DURING ROMAN RULE

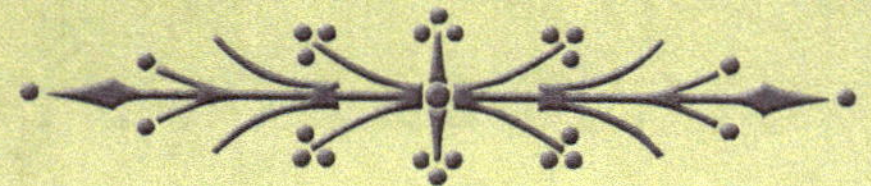

The Romans officially conquered Greece in 146 Bc. However, they didn't gain control over the country of Egypt until much later in 31 Bc. Many historians mark this date as the end of the Hellenistic Period. Despite the fact that they were now under Roman rule, life in Greece didn't change much. The language of the Greeks was the main one used in the eastern region of the Roman Empire for centuries afterwards.

Now you know more about the history of Ancient Greece and the factors that led up to the fall of this great civilization. You can find more History books from Baby Professor by searching the website of your favorite book retailer.

Visit
BABY PROFESSOR
EDUCATION KIDS
www.BabyProfessorBooks.com
to download Free Baby Professor eBooks
and view our catalog of new and exciting
Children's Books